Two and Three

By Theresa Kim

Illustrated by Ann Iosa

Target Skill Classify/Categorize

PEARSON

Scott
Foresman

Meg and Ed are
on the sand.

Ed can dig up two shells.

Meg can dig up
three shells.

Ed can see two birds
on the sand.

Meg can see three birds
on a hill.

Ed can see two frogs.

Meg can see three frogs.